PRACTICE B

SIGNATURES

All Smiles

Harcourt Brace & Company

Orlando Atlanta Austin Boston San Francisco Chicago Dallas New York Toronto London

CONTENTS

ALL SMILES

Printed in the United States of America

ISBN 0-15-307412-4

8 9 10   030   99

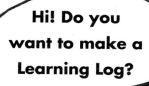

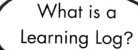

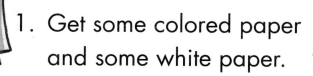

1. Get some colored paper and some white paper.

2. Staple the paper to make a book.

3. Write *My Learning Log*. Then write your name and draw some pictures on the cover.

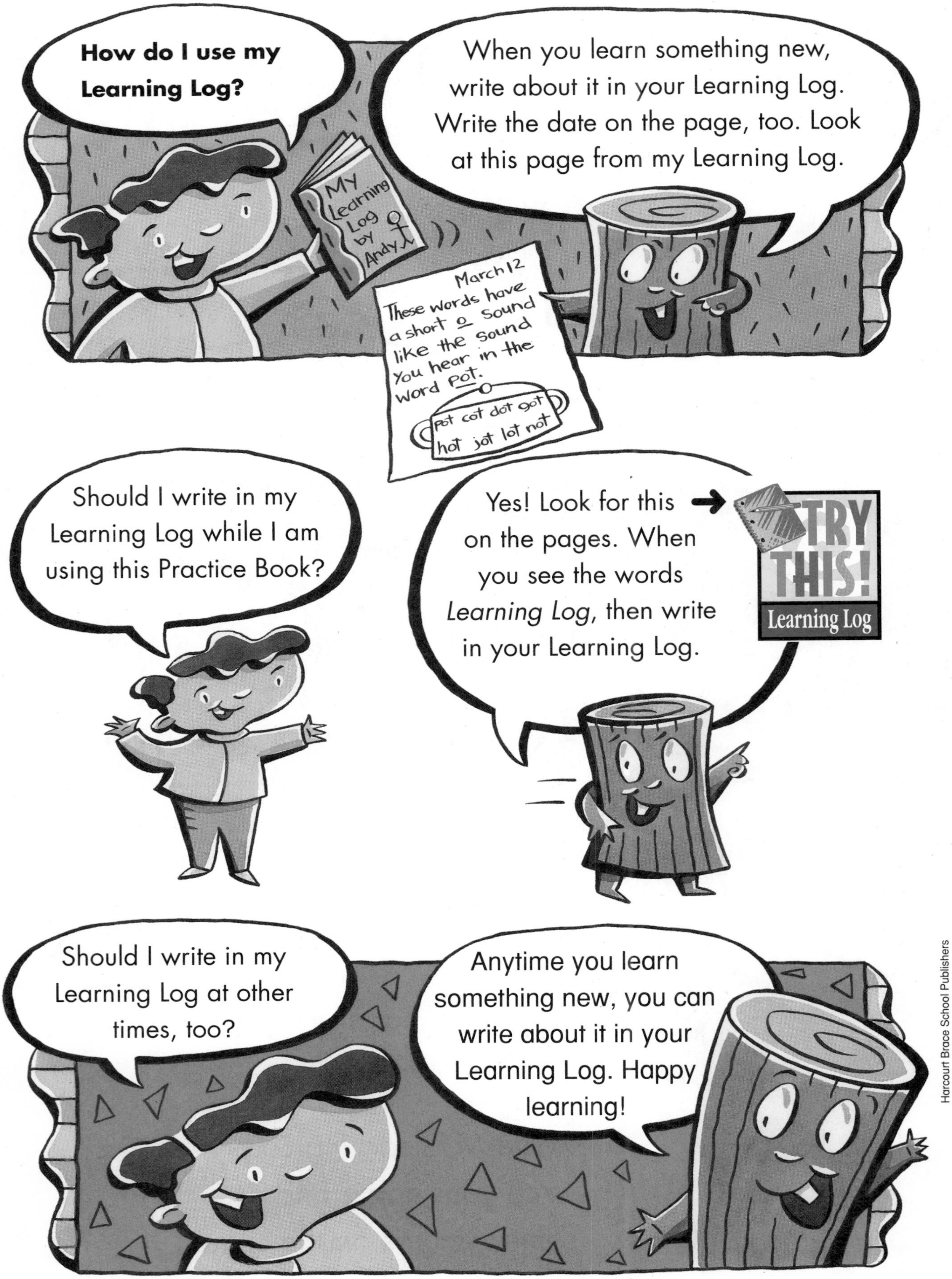
How do I use my Learning Log?
When you learn something new, write about it in your Learning Log. Write the date on the page, too. Look at this page from my Learning Log.
My Learning Log by Andy
March 12
These words have a short o sound like the sound you hear in the word pot.
pot cot dot got hot jot lot not
Should I write in my Learning Log while I am using this Practice Book?
Yes! Look for this on the pages. When you see the words *Learning Log*, then write in your Learning Log.
TRY THIS! Learning Log
Should I write in my Learning Log at other times, too?
Anytime you learn something new, you can write about it in your Learning Log. Happy learning!

Cut out the words. Add more words, and make your own sentences. Glue your sentences onto a sheet of paper.

For me	We were	My shadow
Today	At school	Someone
Wait	! !	Made

Away from the street

Trapped	Big	Grew
. . .	I	You	A play city

my shadow	we were	for me
someone	at school	today
made		!	!	wait
away from the street
grew		big	trapped
a play city	you	I	.	.	.

Harcourt Brace School Publishers

Name _____

Complete the story frame.

Before the Paper Mouse Falls

Roberto can't sleep.

When the Paper Mouse Falls

The mouse casts a big shadow.

After the Paper Mouse Falls

The dog gets scared.

Harcourt Brace School Publishers

Name _____

Some **describing words** tell how things are different. Add **er** to tell how two things are different. Add **est** to tell how more than two things are different.

Write the word that best completes each sentence.

1. I have a _____ shadow.

small   smallest

2. My shadow is _____ than before.

small   smaller

3. I have the _____ shadow of all!

big   biggest

Name _____

A. Write the Spelling Words in their correct shapes. Color the boxes that have the letter *a*.

1.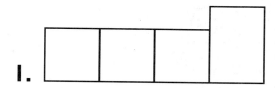

2.

3.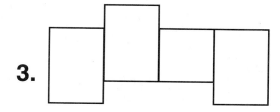

4.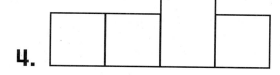

B. Write two Spelling Words to complete the rhyme.

We saw you play in the <u>game</u>.

Everybody _____!

I could have watched all <u>day</u>.

Was it fun to _____?

Read the rhyme. Circle the words that have the same vowel sound you hear in *snake*. Then write each word where it belongs.

One hot day
A snake did say,

I'll take a train
To the lake today.
I can not wait
To play and swim.
If it doesn't rain,
I'll jump right in!

ay	ai	a–e

How are the words that you wrote alike? How are they different?

Harcourt Brace School Publishers

Name _____

Write the word that best completes each sentence.

1. Do you like to _____?

      hop   hopped   hopping

2. I love _____!

      hop   hopped   hopping

3. I never feel like _____.

      stop   stopped   stopping

4. One time I _____ all day.

      hop   hopped   hopping

5. At last, I _____.

      stop   stopped   stopping

TRY THIS!
Learning Log

How did *hop* change to *hopped* and *hopping*? How did *stop* change? Write about it.

Name _____

Read each animal riddle. Write the name of the animal.

This animal is very big.
It lives in the water.
But it is not a fish.

_____

- - - - - - - - - - - - - - - - -

_____

This animal can climb.
It has a long tail.
It lives in the tops of trees.

_____

- - - - - - - - - - - - - - - - -

_____

bird

This animal can hop fast.
It has a small tail.
It eats in my garden!

_____

- - - - - - - - - - - - - - - - -

_____

rabbit

monkey

This animal sits on a branch.
It makes a nest.
It can fly up high.

_____

- - - - - - - - - - - - - - - - -

_____

whale

Harcourt Brace School Publishers

ALL SMILES Practice Book

Name _____

Write the word that best completes each sentence.

started	scrubbed	eyes	take	never

1. I have to _____ a bath.

2. I _____ like to take one!

3. Pig _____ her bath.

4. She shut her _____

and _____ all over.

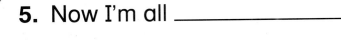

shaking	steps	part	done

5. Now I'm all _____.

6. I'm _____ off the water!

7. This is the best _____.

8. Pig ran down the _____ and into the mud.

Draw a picture of Pig. Write what Pig says. Use some words from the boxes.

Harcourt Brace School Publishers

Name _____

Complete the flowchart to tell about the story.

Henry wants to give Mudge a bath.

Mudge starts to shake.

SCIENCE

Name _____

Some describing words tell about the **weather**.

Look at the weather map. Then write the words to finish the sentences.

_____

- -

1. It's a _____ day in California.

_____

- -

2. Texas is having a _____ day.

_____

- -

3. Today it's _____ in Maine.

_____

- -

4. It's very _____ in Florida.

Harcourt Brace School Publishers

Name _____

A. Write a Spelling Word for each letter problem. Then circle the two letters in each word that are the same.

1. **th + at** = _____

2. **th + en** = _____

3. **th + e** = _____

4. **th + ey** = _____

B. Write two Spelling Words to complete the question. Then draw a picture to answer it.

What will ☐☐ ☐ do

to clean up ☐☐ ☐ dog?

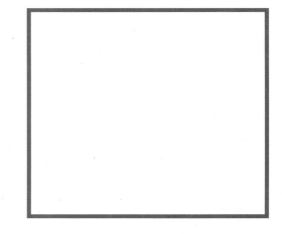

Harcourt Brace School Publishers

Write the words in the puzzles.

1. Spot rides down the hill on a ____.

2. He ____ into an animal.

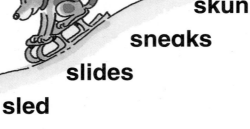

skunk

sneaks

slides

sled

smells

stops

3. Oh, no! The animal is a ____!

4. Now Spot ____ bad.

5. The skunk ____ away.

6. I hope Spot ____ chasing skunks!

TRY THIS!
Learning Log

Look at the words in the puzzles. How are these words alike?
Write more words that begin like these.

Name _____

Write the word that best completes each sentence.

SCIENCE

_____

1. A baby duck is _____ to hatch.

       ran   ready   dear

_____

2. A little _____ pops out.

     head   breath   leaves

_____

3. Baby ducks will _____ their wings.

     fed   spread   read

_____

4. Big ducks like to eat _____.

     beads   bed   bread

Name _____

Write the word that answers each riddle.

snake	hay	whale	tail

I can wag.
I am on a dog.
_____
- - - - - - - - - - - - - - - - - - -
I am a _____.

I look like an *S*.
I hiss.
_____
- - - - - - - - - - - - - - - - - - -
I am a _____.

I live in the sea.
I am very big.
_____
- - - - - - - - - - - - - - - - - - -
I am a _____.

Some animals eat me.
I am yellow.
_____
- - - - - - - - - - - - - - - - - - -
I am _____.

Write a list of words that rhyme with *snake*. Write a riddle for
one word.

Harcourt Brace School Publishers

Name _____

Add *ed* or *ing* to each word. Write the new word that completes each sentence. Write numbers to show the times, too.

| stop | + | p | + | ing | = | stopping |

mop   **scrub**   **hop**   **wag**

1. Ruff was _____ at ☐ o'clock.

hop

2. At ☐ o'clock, Ruff was _____.

mop

3. At ☐ o'clock, Ruff _____ the tub.

scrub

4. Ruff _____ his tail at ☐ o'clock.

wag

Name _____

Write the words in the boxes to complete the sentences.

| front | beaks | teeth | goldfish | food |

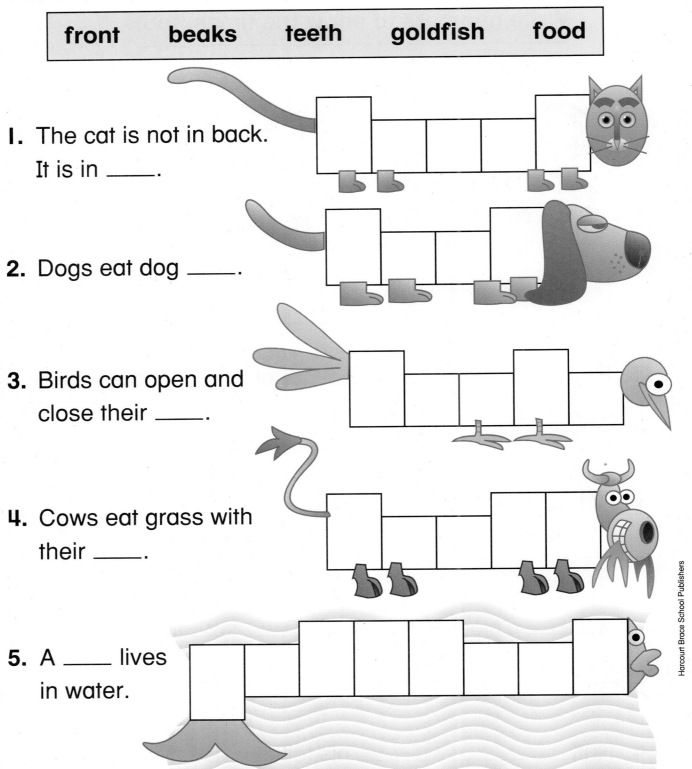

1. The cat is not in back.
It is in ____.

2. Dogs eat dog ____.

3. Birds can open and
close their ____.

4. Cows eat grass with
their ____.

5. A ____ lives
in water.

Harcourt Brace School Publishers

Name _____

| outdoors | seeds | cheeks | also |

6. Chicks eat ___.

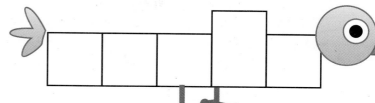

7. Hens ___ eat them.

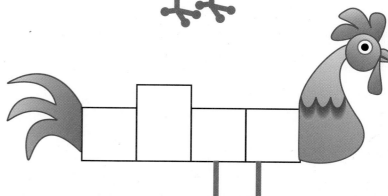

8. A mouse's ___ get big when it eats.

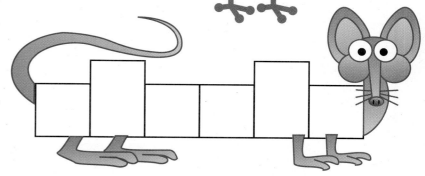

9. Some animals live ___.

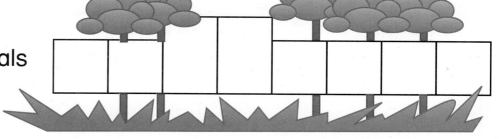

Make your own clues for the words. Then draw the word boxes. Give your sentences and boxes to a classmate to do.

Harcourt Brace School Publishers

Fill in the K-W-L chart.

Pets	
K	**What I Know**
W	**What I Want to Know**
L	**What I Learned**

Name _____

An **action word** tells what someone or something does.

Circle the action words on the award. Then write them. Use some action words to tell about you.

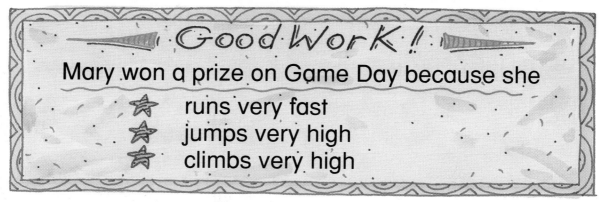

Good Work!

Mary won a prize on Game Day because she

⭐ runs very fast
⭐ jumps very high
⭐ climbs very high

I. Write three words that tell what Mary does well.

_____   _____   _____
- - - - - - - - - - -   - - - - - - - - - - -   - - - - - - - - - - -
_____   _____   _____

2. Now write about you.

     _____   _____
     - - - - - - - - - - - - - - - -   - - - - - - - - - - -

I can _____ . I _____ very well.

_____

- -

I _____ very well, too.

TRY THIS!
Writing

Draw a picture to show what you can do well. Write a sentence to go with it.

Harcourt Brace School Publishers

Name _____

A. Write Spelling Words to complete the rhyme.

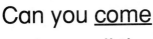

have   live   do   some

Can you <u>come</u>
and see all the pets?

_____
- -

There are _____
that are flying jets!

Look at the dog
and the rabbits, <u>too</u>.
What is that frog

_____
- -

going to _____?

B. Write Spelling Words to complete the sentence.

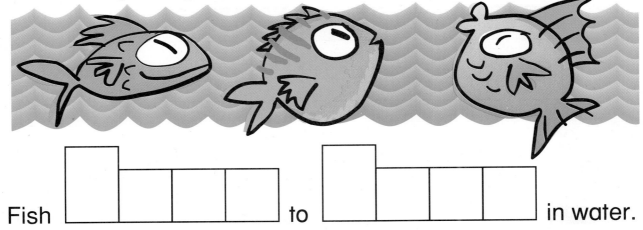

Fish ☐☐☐☐ to ☐☐☐☐ in water.

Name _____

Read the poem. Circle the words that have the same vowel sound as *beak*. Then write each word where it belongs.

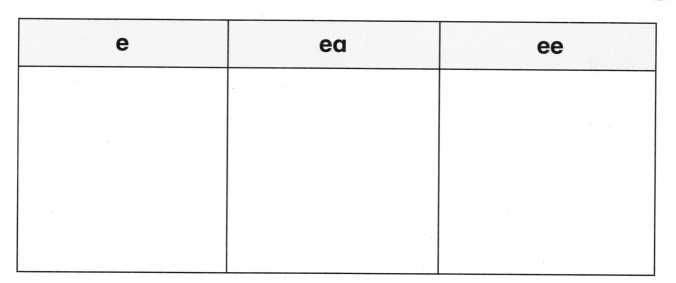

I can't sleep.
I need some sheep.
One, two, three,
Where can they be?
I want to dream
About food we can eat!
So I'll shut each eye and close my beak.
Now you can say "Good night" to me!

e	ea	ee

How are the words on the chart alike? Write other words you know that are like these words.

Say each word and picture name together to make a new word. Write the new word on the lines. Then use the words to complete the sentences.

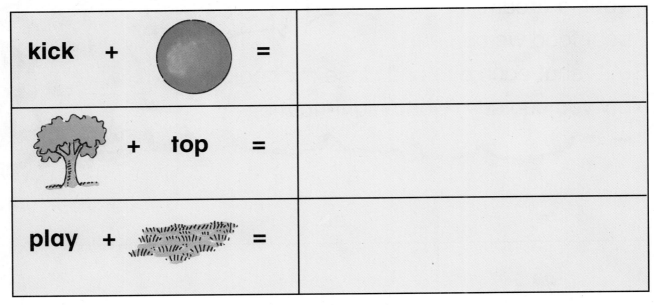

kick + ⬤ =	
tree + top =	
play + 🟤 =	

_____
- -

1. Ann went to the _____.

_____
- -

2. Next, she played _____.

_____
- -

3. The ball got stuck in the _____.

Harcourt Brace School Publishers

**Cut out the rockets and rocket cones.
Match the words to the sentences. Glue
the pairs together on a sheet of paper.**

I have _____ here before.

Shut the _____.

I will _____ you my school.

We must _____.

Can we _____ go now?

It is _____ to be back!

Let's blast off into _____.

We _____ not get back in time.

Who _____ the books?

may

door

took

show

been

hurry

great

please

space

Harcourt Brace School Publishers

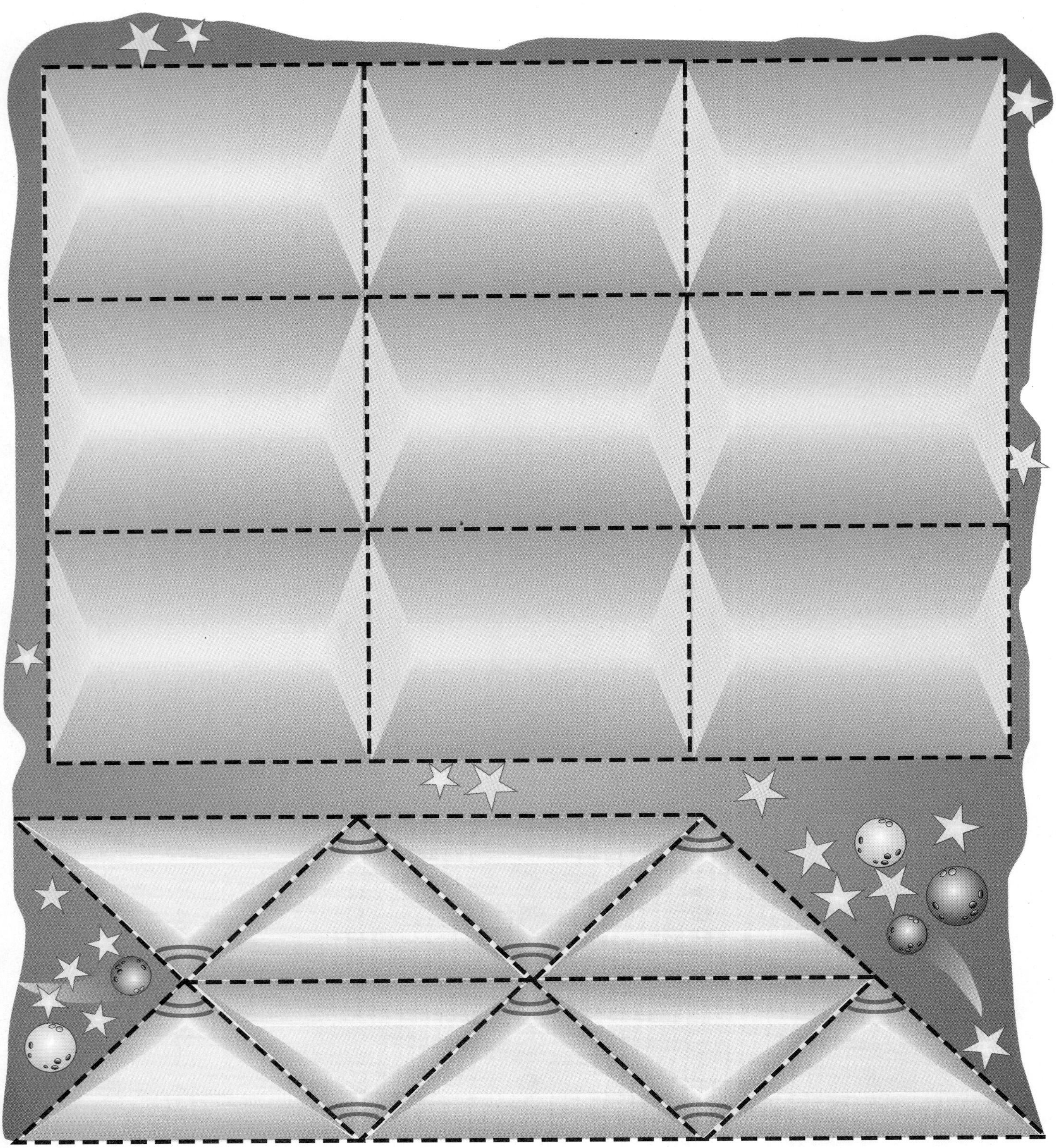

Name _____

Finish the story frame.

Beginning

Middle

Ending

An **action word** can tell **about the past**. Some action words that tell about the past end with the letters *ed.*

Circle and write the action words that tell about the past.

1. A spaceship landed on the ground.

2. The door opened.

3. I climbed up the steps.

4. A green cat wanted to be friends!

Harcourt Brace School Publishers

Name _____

A. Write a Spelling Word to complete each sentence. Color the box that has the letter *e*. Then draw a face to go with the sentence.

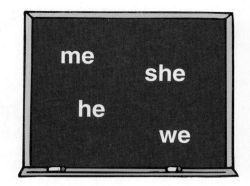

1. To tell about a girl, say 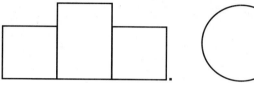.

2. To tell about a boy, say 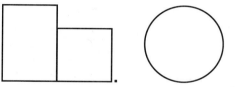.

3. To tell about yourself, say .

4. To tell about all of us, say 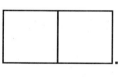.

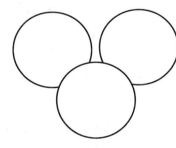

B. Write a sentence using two of your Spelling Words.

_____

_____

_____

_____

Name _____

Write the word that best completes each sentence.

bows   show   grow   rainbow   rows

1. I have something to _____ you.

2. This is what I _____ in my garden!

3. I planted gifts in _____.

4. I also planted lots of big _____.

5. My garden is like a _____.

TRY THIS! Learning Log

Write *grow*, *coat*, and *joke*. What is the same about these words? What is different?

Name _____

Write the word that fits the sentence and has the vowel sound you hear in *steak*.

1. Zin and Yon took a lunch _____.

break   time   beak

2. They had some _____ food to eat.

good   great   weigh

3. They ate some _____.

stack   food   steak

4. Then they had _____ plums.

eight   break   two

5. Did they gain any _____?

sleigh   time   weight

TRY THIS!
Learning Log

Write *weight* and *steak*. How are these words alike? How are they different?

Name _____

Read the story. Circle the words with the same vowel sound as *day*. Write them in the correct column.

Land Snails

You may think that all snails are the same. There are many kinds. These are land snails. They like rain and they like to live in wet places. They like to stay in the shade. You might see some snails in the day or late at night.

ai	ay	a-e

Name _____

Put the planets together. Match the words to the clues.

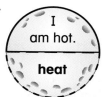

I am not close to you.

Two words are in me.

I keep water cold.

I am hot.

I am *not* hot.

I shine at night.

Find *round* in me.

I go to your house.

GO ON

cold | around

visit | far

ice | heat

star | maybe

Write each word in the chart where it belongs.

| heat | star | maybe | ice |
| visit | around | cold | far |

Rhymes with *jar*	Has Five Letters
Things You Feel	**Ends with the Letter *d***

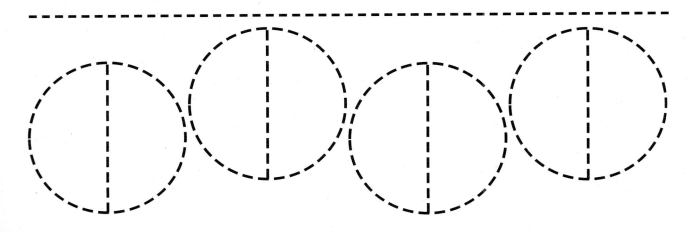

Harcourt Brace School Publishers

Name _____

Fill in the K-W-L chart.

PLANETS
K–What I Know
W–What I Want to Know
L–What I Learned

Harcourt Brace School Publishers

An **action word** can tell **about now**. The letter *s* is added to some action words that tell about now.

Write an action word to finish each sentence.

run
wave
yell
runs
eats
steps
jumps
waves
yells
swims

1. Penny _____ out into the new world.

2. She _____ in the red water.

3. The animals _____ to her.

4. She _____ all the food.

5. Now she _____ to her friends.

TRY THIS!
Talking Tip

Work with a friend. Act out something you can do. Have a friend guess the action word and use it in a sentence.

Harcourt Brace School Publishers

Name _____

A. Read the Spelling Words and name the pictures. Write the word that rhymes with each picture. Circle the letter *i* in each word.

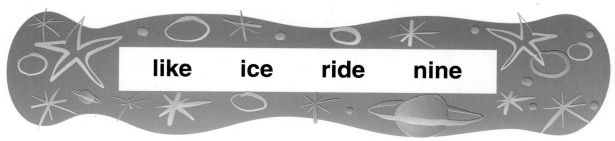

| like | ice | ride | nine |

bike
1. _____

mice
2. _____

hide
3. _____

B. Write a Spelling Word in the puzzle to tell about the picture.

| p | i | n | e | s |

Name _____

Write the word that best completes each sentence.

| far | Mars | star | part | hard |

The Planet _____

_____

1. Mars is very _____ away.

2. It is not _____ to see it in the sky.

3. Mars looks like a red _____.

4. No one has found life on any _____ of Mars.

Write *fan* and *far* and read these words aloud. Listen to the middle sounds. What is different about the sounds in these words?

Harcourt Brace School Publishers

ALL SMILES Practice Book

Name _____

Read the story. Then answer the questions.

The New Planet

Jack found a new planet. It looks like a big box. The plants are blue. The sky is green with red dots. It snows all the time. Maybe you can go there someday.

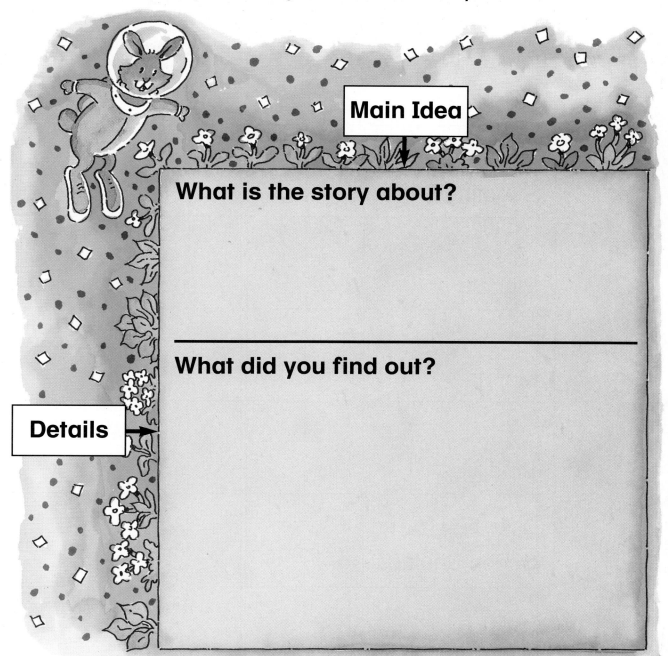

Main Idea

What is the story about?

_____

What did you find out?

Details

Name _____

Count the things you see in the night sky. Color a box on the graph for each. Then answer the questions.

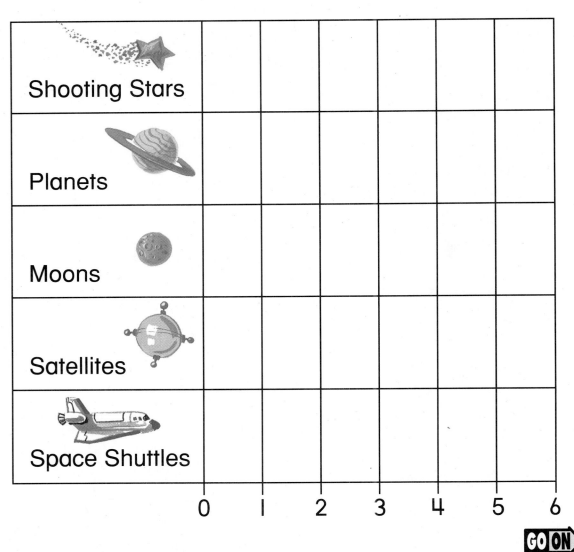

	0	1	2	3	4	5	6
Shooting Stars							
Planets							
Moons							
Satellites							
Space Shuttles							

GO ON

Name _____

MATH

1. Which row has the most?

_____

- -

_____

2. Which has the least?

_____

- -

_____

3. Are there more moons or more planets?

_____

- -

_____

4. What other things does the graph tell you?

_____

- -

_____

_____

- -

_____

Name _____

Write the word or words that best complete each sentence.

How to Make a Spaceship

1. Get an _____ box.

2. Make a _____.

3. _____ in and _____ on tight!

4. Now it's time to _____.

hold

ramp

land

Jump

old

What can you make from a box? Write how to make it.

Harcourt Brace School Publishers

Name _____

Write the word that best completes each sentence.

REVIEW PETE'S PLACE RESTAURANT

Today's Specials ~
Tender Brisket 2.10 Reuben Loaf 1.96
Cinnamon Rolls 3.50 Vegetarian 2.50

snapped

nice **screaming** **mean**

Monday October 23 35 cents

A Great Place to Eat

My friend and I found a great new place to eat! It all started at lunchtime.

"Let's go out to eat! Let's go out to eat!"

_____

my friend kept _____.

_____

"I _____ it!"

_____

At last, I _____. "All right! I'll go," I said. Now I am glad we went. We

_____

found a _____ place to eat named Pete's Place.

GO ON

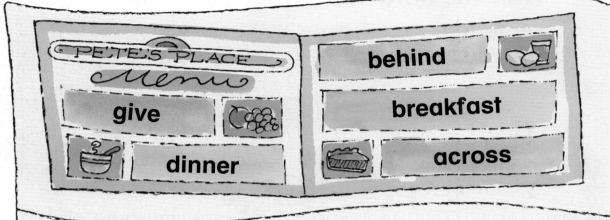

Pete's Place is a great place for

_____   _____

------------------------   ------------------------

_____, lunch, or _____.

_____

The workers _____ you good food! Pete's

_____

Place is right _____ the hat shop and

_____

_____ from the school. I hope you go

there soon!

Make a menu for Pete's Place. Write a list of things you might eat there.

Name _____

Think about how Geraldine's feelings changed in the story. Then complete the story map.

How Geraldine Feels at the Beginning

What Makes Geraldine Change?

How Geraldine Feels at the End

The words **is** and **are** tell about now.
Use *is* to tell about one person, place, or thing.
Use *are* to tell about more than one person, place, or thing.

Write *is* or *are* to finish each sentence. Then circle the picture that answers the riddle.

_____
- - - - - - - - - - - - - - - -

1. Ron _____ very little.

_____
- - - - - - - - - - - - - - - -

2. Ron's eyes _____ blue.

_____
- - - - - - - - - - - - - - - -

3. His two feet _____ small.

_____
- - - - - - - - - - - - - - - -

4. Ron _____ a baby.
Which baby is Ron?

Make up a riddle. Use the words *is* and *are* to tell it. Ask a friend to guess what the answer is.

Harcourt Brace School Publishers

Name _____

A. Circle the Spelling Word hidden in each word. Then write the word in its shape.

1. this

2. seesaw

3. forgive

4. wasp

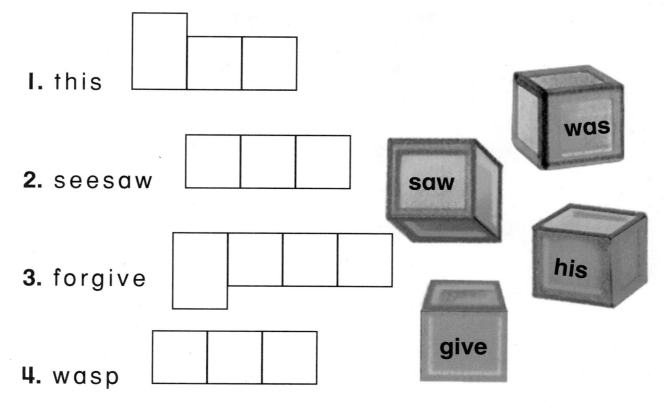

B. Write the two Spelling Words to complete the sentences.

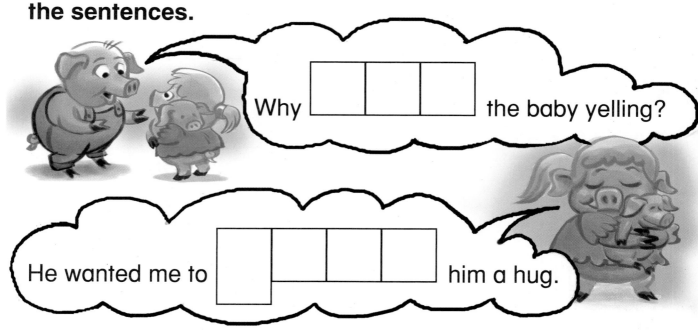

Why ☐☐☐ the baby yelling?

He wanted me to ☐☐☐☐ him a hug.

Read the make-believe breakfast cereal offer.
Then fill in the form.

A Free Gift from Fun Flakes

Get your very own free spinning top.
Just fill out the form. Then mail it
with two UPC codes. You will get
your free top in about three weeks.

Name _____

Street _____

City _____ **State** _____

Zip Code _____

Cut a sheet of paper in the shape of an envelope. Make up an address
for *Fun Flakes,* and write it on the envelope. Write your name and
address in the top left corner. Draw a stamp, too.

Harcourt Brace School Publishers

Name _____

Add the letters *ed* or *ing* to the word to complete each sentence.

> **hop + p + ing = hopping**

_____
- - - - - - - - - - - - - - - - - - -

1. Begin by _____ on one leg.

hop

_____
- - - - - - - - - - - - - - - - - - -

2. You almost _____ on my toe!

hop

_____
- - - - - - - - - - - - - - - - - - -

3. Next, start _____ your
hands.   clap

_____
- - - - - - - - - - - - - - - - - - -

4. Stop! You _____ too much!

clap

_____
- - - - - - - - - - - - - - - - - - -

5. Now you may begin _____
and hopping.   hum

Harcourt Brace School Publishers

Write the word that best completes each sentence and has the same vowel sound as *street*.

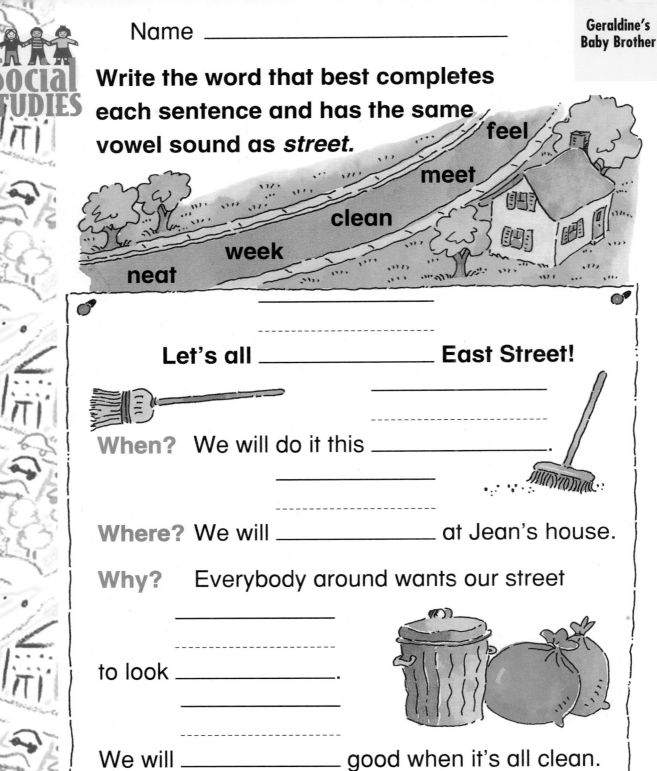

feel

meet

clean

week

neat

_____

Let's all _____ East Street!

When? We will do it this _____.

Where? We will _____ at Jean's house.

Why? Everybody around wants our street

_____

to look _____.

We will _____ good when it's all clean.

TRY THIS!
Word Play

Write the word *street*. Make three other words, using some of the letters in *street*.

Cut out, fold, and read the newspaper stories. Write the main idea of each one. Draw a line under each detail.

fold

The Biggest Cake in Town

Joe Baker baked the biggest cake Fun Town has ever seen! It is almost as big as a house. The cake is very good. You can see the cake at Joe's Bake Shop.

Main Idea:

Fun Town News

Baby Bear Drives a Car

A baby bear was seen driving a car down Fun Street. Everyone came out to see him. His friends waved at him. He was having a good time!

Main Idea:

fold

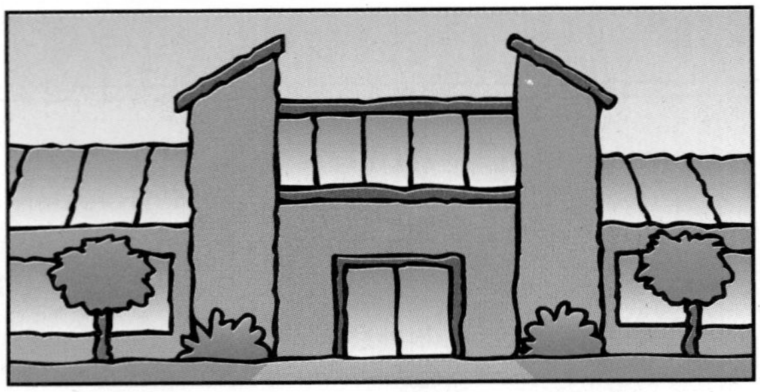

New School Is Done at Last

Red Creek School is done. The inside is nice and bright. The playground is very big. The school will open very soon. You will like the new school.

Main Idea:

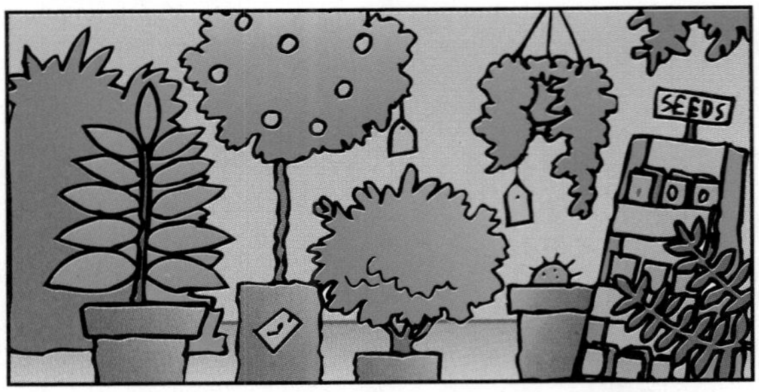
SEEDS

It's a Big Sale!

Come to the big sale at the Garden Shop. All the plants are on sale. The trees are on sale, too. Even the seeds have been marked down. Hurry and come today!

Main Idea:

Name _____

Write the words to complete the riddles.

_____

1. Mary and I _____ it.

   smiled   scary   shared

_____

2. We _____ when we rode on it.

   cubes   other   smiled

_____

3. It is _____ that goes up and down.

   other   something   left

_____

4. It is not _____ at all.

   scary   tasted   other

_____

5. It is a _____.

   something   cube   swing

Harcourt Brace School Publishers

_____

1. There were some _____ in my glass.

       smiled   swing   left

_____

2. They _____ like water.

     tasted   smiled   other

_____

3. You can see them in water and _____ things.

      swing   other   left

_____

4. They are ice _____.

    scary   swing   cubes

TRY THIS! Writing

Write a food riddle. Use the word *tasted* in it. Let a partner read your riddle and guess it.

Harcourt Brace School Publishers

Name _____

Complete the story map to show how Julius changes in the story.

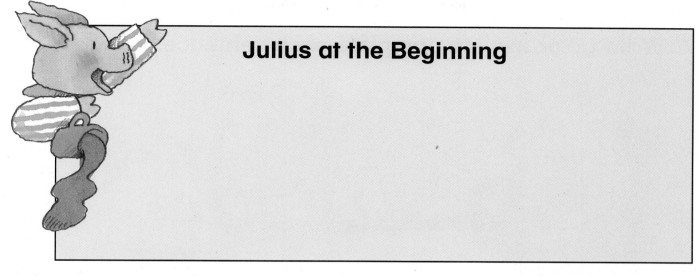

Julius at the Beginning

Things That Make Julius Change

Julius at the End

Harcourt Brace School Publishers

The word **go** tells about now.
The word **went** tells about the past.

A. Write *go* or *went* to complete each sentence.

_____
- -
1. Last night, the pigs _____ to dinner.

_____
- -
2. Now, the pigs _____ to breakfast.

_____
- -
3. Last week, the pigs _____ to school.

_____
- - - - - - - - - - - - - - -
4. Now, they _____ to the beach.

Name _____

B. Finish these sentences with your own words and *go* and *went*.

1. The pigs _____

_____

_____

_____

_____

2. On their birthday the pigs _____

_____

_____

_____

_____

3. Last week they _____.

Where did you go yesterday? Where do you go after school?
Write about it.

A. Write a Spelling Word to complete each sentence.

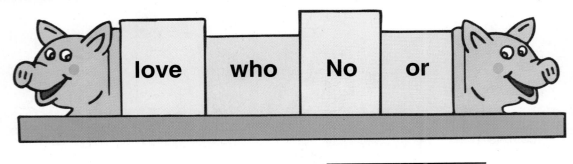

love | who | No | or

_____

1. Do you like to read about pigs _____ dogs?

_____

2. I _____ to read about pigs.

_____

3. Do you know _____ took my pig book?

_____

4. _____, but I will help you find it.

B. Circle the Spelling Word hidden in each word. Then write the word in its shape. Color the box that has the letter *o*.

1. whoever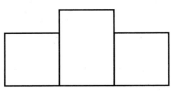

2. for

Harcourt Brace School Publishers

Name _____

Write the words to complete the sentences.

_____

- -

1. My _____ looks just like me.

_____

- -

2. You will look _____ when you see us.

_____

- -

3. She likes to _____ in the water.

_____

- -

4. I like to _____ in the park.

_____

- -

5. We both like to feed the _____.

How are the words you wrote alike? Write some more words like these.

Harcourt Brace School Publishers

Name _____

Write the words to complete the word problem. Then write the number that tells what is left.

cube
huge
used
mule
cubes

_____

- -

1. I had three ice _____.

_____

- -

2. I gave away one _____ cube.

_____

- - - - - - - - - - - - - - - - - - - -

3. My _____ wanted it.

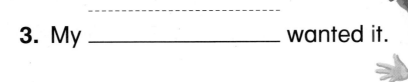

_____

- - - - - - - - - - - - - - - - - - - -

4. I _____ another cube in my water.

_____

- - - - - - - - - - - - - - - - - - - -

5. Now I have ☐ ice _____ left.

Harcourt Brace School Publishers

Name _____

Write the words to complete the riddle.

grow   know   low

slow

crow

_____

1. I _____ in an egg.

2. I _____ how to fly.

3. I can fly fast or _____.

4. I can fly high or _____.

5. I am a _____.

Write __ow__ on a sheet of paper. Write the letters _b_, _l_, _m_, _r_, _sh_, and _gl_ on small squares. Make as many words as you can. Write the words.

Name _____

Write the words to complete the letter.

stove   slept   smelled

small   spot

Dear Grandpa,

_____

- -

Mom and I _____ in a tent last

_____

- -

night. We picked a nice _____.

_____

- -

We made dinner on a _____

_____

- -

_____.

_____

- -

The food _____ good.

Name _____

snack   **story**   **stars**
sleep   **sky**

_____

After dinner, Mom told me a _____.

Then we looked up at the

_____   _____

_____ in the _____.

_____

We ate one _____ and went

_____

to _____. It was fun!

Love,
Meg

TRY THIS!
Word Play

Write the words in the pencils on cards. Cut the cards after the first two
letters. Mix up the pieces. Then put the words together.

Read what Scott is saying. Then answer the questions.

My mom drives a school bus. She likes her job a lot. I ride on her bus every day. I always sit up front with my friends. It's fun to have Mom take me to school.

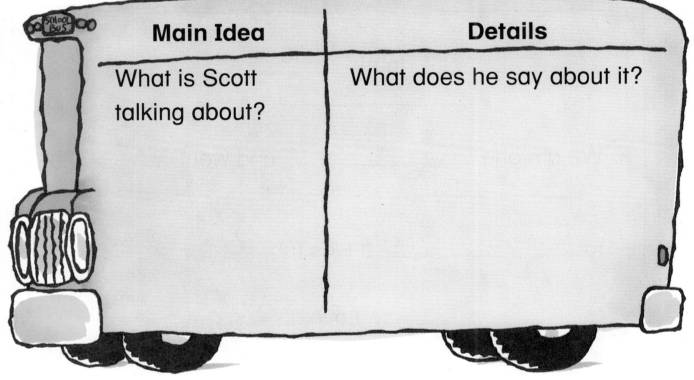

Main Idea	Details
What is Scott talking about?	What does he say about it?

TRY THIS! Writing

Write about a job you would like to have. Circle your main idea. Draw lines under the details.

Name _____

Write the words to complete the letter.

slept   children   letter

week   beach

Dear Grandma,

_____

I got your _____. Last

_____

_____ we went to the

_____

_____. I had fun playing with the

_____

other _____. At night I

_____

_____ in my very own room!

GO ON

Name _____

pretty   **feeding**   **rose**

skirt

_____

I had fun _____ the fish.

_____

I picked a _____ in the

_____

garden. It was very _____.

_____

The blue _____ you sent fits me.
I like it a lot.

Love,
Maria

Write a letter to a friend. In your letter, use some of the words that
you wrote.

Name _____

Complete the story map.

What is Silvia's gift?	What is the problem?

How does Silvia use the gift?

What happens at the end?

Harcourt Brace School Publishers

SUMMARIZE AND RETELL   **69**

The words **was** and **were** tell about the past. Use **was** to tell about one person, place, or thing. Use **were** to tell about more than one person, place, or thing.

Write *was* or *were* to complete each sentence. Then write the number of friends in all.

_____

1. My friend Marco _____ in my house today.

_____

2. Jason and Lee _____ in the front yard.

_____

3. Tara _____ in the back yard.

_____

4. There _____ ☐ friends in all at my house.

Name _____

A. Read the Spelling Words and name the pictures. Write the word that rhymes with each picture. Circle the letter *o* in each word.

| old | rose | home | go |

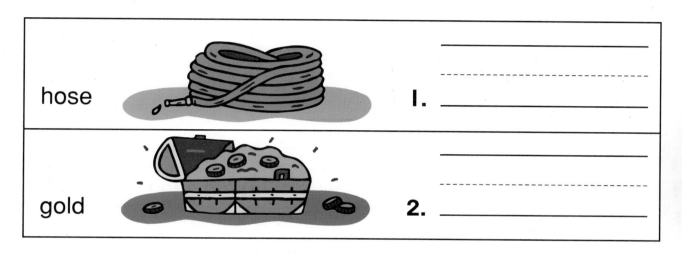

hose   1. _____

gold   2. _____

B. Solve each letter problem. Write the Spelling Word in the shape box.

1. **told – t** =

2. **homework – work** =

3. **ago – a** =

Follow the directions.

1. Draw a star by the neat writing. Why should you use your best writing on a test?

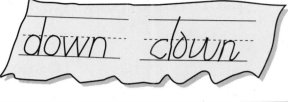

_____

_____

_____

_____

2. Some tests have circles to fill in. Draw a line under the best filled circle.

1. Ⓐ Ⓑ Ⓒ Ⓓ
2. Ⓐ ⬤ Ⓒ Ⓓ

3. Directions tell you what to do on a test. Read the directions. How do you know that *bread* is not the right answer?

Circle the word that completes each sentence and has the same vowel sound as *make*.

1. I like to eat ___bread___ .

bread   cake   take

_____

_____

_____

_____

Make a word wheel. Work with a classmate to read the new words. Take turns making up a sentence for each word.

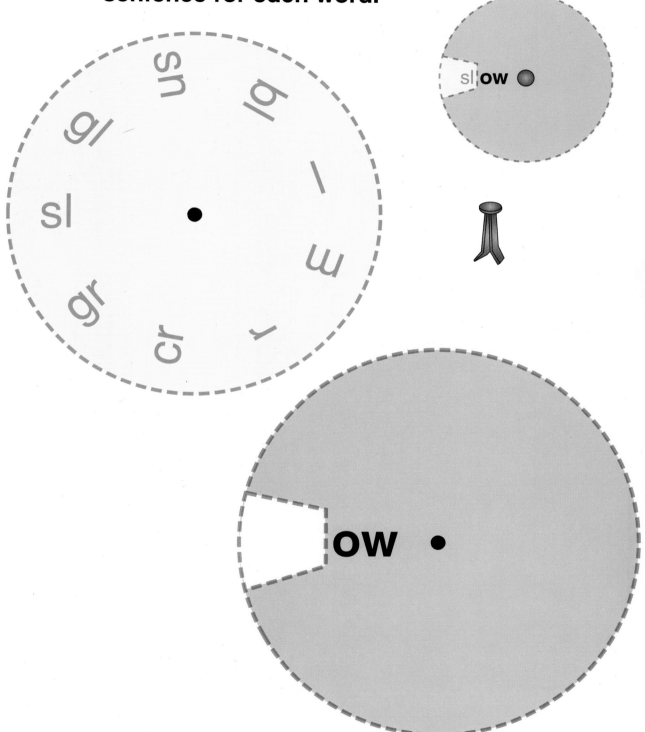

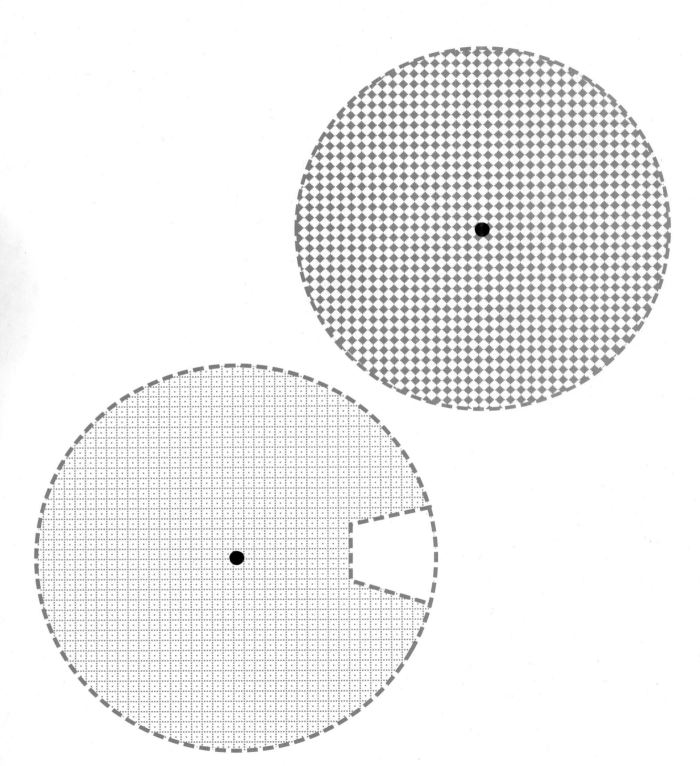

Harcourt Brace School Publishers

Name _____

Write the words to complete the ad.

scarves	sleds	snacks
skip	snow	

Snow Shop Sale

_____
- -

Come to the _____ shop sale.

_____
- -

We have lots of _____ and

_____
- -

_____.

_____
- -

We will give away free _____.

_____
- -

Don't _____ this sale!

TRY THIS! Writing

Imagine that you have your own shop. What kind of shop is it?
What do you sell? Write an ad for your shop.

INITIAL CLUSTERS WITH *s*   **75**

Name _____

Write the words to complete the riddles.

need   tree   green

leaves   read

_____

1. I have a lot of _____ on me.

2. They are _____.

3. I _____ light and water to grow.

4. Everybody likes to sit and _____ next to me.

5. I am a big _____.

LONG VOWEL: /ē/ea, ee   ALL SMILES Practice Book

Harcourt Brace School Publishers

Name _____

see

teeth

peach

eat

sweet

_____
- - - - - - - - - - - - - - -

1. I am something to _____.

_____
- - - - - - - - - - - - - - -

2. You bite into me with your _____.

_____
- - - - - - - - - - - - - - -

3. I taste _____.

_____
- - - - - - - - - - - - - - -

4. You can _____ me in a tree.

_____
- - - - - - - - - - - - - - -

5. I am a _____.

TRY THIS!
Writing

Think of something that is sweet to eat. Write a riddle for it.

SKILLS AND STRATEGIES INDEX

How to make a Learning Log 1–2

DECODING
Phonic analysis
  Consonant correspondences
    Clusters, initial
      with *s* 16, 64–65, 75
      with *w* 61
    Clusters, final
      -ld, *-mp*, *-nd* 44
  Vowel correspondences
    /ā/*ai*, *ay*, *a-e* 8, 18, 34
    /ā/*ea*, *ei(gh)* 33
    /är/*ar* 40
    /e/*ea* 17
    /ē/*e* 25
    /ē/*ea*, *ee* 25, 52, 76–77
    /ō/*ow* 32, 63, 73–74
    /yōō/*u-e* 62
Structural analysis
  Inflections
    -ed, *-ing* 9, 19, 51

VOCABULARY
Compound words 26
Key Words 3–4, 11–12, 20–21, 27–28,
  35–36, 45–46, 55–56, 67–68

COMPREHENSION
Drawing conclusions 10
Main idea and details 41, 53–54, 66
Summarize and retell 5, 13, 22, 29, 37,
  47, 57, 69

STUDY SKILLS
Forms 50
Graphs 42–43
Test-taking strategies 72

GRAMMAR
Action words 23
  about now 38
  about the past 30
Describing words
  with *-er*, *-est* 6
  for weather 14
Go and *went* 58–59
Is and *are* 48
Was and *were* 70

SPELLING
Words with
  long *a* 7
  long *e* 31
  long *i* 39
  long *o* 71
  th 15
More words to remember 24, 49
More words to remember with *o* 60